Books by Oxford Scientific Films

BEES AND HONEY
Photographs by David Thompson

THE BUTTERFLY CYCLE
Photographs by Dr. John Cooke

HOUSE MOUSE
Photographs by David Thompson

THE SPIDER'S WEB
Photographs by Dr. John Cooke

The Stickleback Cycle

By Oxford Scientific Films

Photographs by David Thompson

G. P. Putnam's Sons New York

First American Edition 1979

Printed by Toppan Printing Co. Singapore

Library of Congress Cataloging in Publication Data
Oxford Scientific Films.
The stickleback cycle.
SUMMARY: Describes the characteristics and behavior of
the most common freshwater fish found in northern
temperate climates.
1. Three-spined stickleback–Behavior–Juvenile literature.
2. Parental behavior in animals–Juvenile literature.
[1. Three-spined stickleback. 2. Fishes]
1. Thompson, David. 1945-II. Title.
QL638.G27093 1979 597'.53 77-28754
ISBN 0-399-20638-8

The Stickleback Cycle

The three-spine stickleback is one of the most common freshwater fish to be found in northern temperate climates. It lives in rivers, lakes and ponds (except for those in mountainous regions), as well as in salt water estuaries and rock pools.

A stickleback can grow to 100mm ($3\frac{7}{8}$ inches) long, but most measure less than 60mm ($2\frac{3}{8}$ inches). They have three dorsal spines in front of the dorsal fin. Both sexes are similarly colored—the upper parts blue-black or green, with paler colors below—but the head of the male is slightly larger in proportion to the body.

Out of the breeding season, sticklebacks are found in mixed schools of males and females. But in the spring, the adult male leaves the school and assumes his breeding colors. His throat and belly turn bright red, and his eyes electric blue. The scales of the dorsal surface become translucent, so that when sexually aroused the male glows in a strangely beautiful way.

The male stickleback chooses a territory in shallow water, attacking any other red-colored males that approach (in this way invisible boundaries are established between adjacent territories).

He selects a site for his nest, and begins excavating a small depression in the sand or mud. He does this by sucking up minute quantities of the substance into his mouth, then swimming away a few centimeters (about 2 inches) before ejecting it.

Having formed a suitable depression, the stickleback starts to build the nest. He painstakingly collects strands of fine weed or algae, prodding them into place with his snout. Each new piece of weed is glued into position by a sticky secretion from the stickleback's kidneys.

The completed nest usually measures about 40mm ($1\frac{1}{2}$ inches) in length and width, filling the depression and projecting slightly above it. It is tunnel-shaped and open at both ends.

The male stickleback recognizes the pregnant female by her spawn-swollen abdomen. As soon as one arrives in his territory, the elaborate courtship ritual begins.

Normally, the first thing a male does on sighting the female is to squeeze his way through the nest, from one end to the other, making certain that it is clear for the female to enter.

That done, the male starts to perform his courtship dance. This takes the form of a series of zigzag approaches toward the female, ending each time with the male heading back in the direction of his nest.

If, after a number of these approaches, the female fails to respond, the male stickleback may well attack her. Usually, however, the female is sufficiently enticed by the zigzag dance to follow the male back to the nest.

The female stickleback will inspect the nest by poking her snout into the entrance; but she will not necessarily go in. Indeed, the courtship procedure may have to be repeated several times before she finally decides to enter.

Getting into the narrow tunnel-shaped nest is quite a struggle for the bloated female. Once there, she takes up a position with her head just inside the exit and her tail sticking out of the entrance.

The male now switches to a new pattern of behavior: he puts his snout against the base of the female's projecting tail and quivers violently. The female gradually begins to lift her tail—a sign that she is about to spawn or lay her eggs.

Then, with her tail raised high, and still being stimulated by the male, the female stickleback releases a stream of between 50 to 100 eggs.

As soon as the last egg is laid the female leaves the nest. Immediately, the male swims through it without stopping, discharging a cloud of sperm as he passes over the eggs. Fertilization thus takes place in the nest.

After spawning, the abdomen of the female becomes concave and she is no longer attractive to the male. So he chases her out of his territory. When her ovaries have developed more ripe eggs she will spawn again.

Meanwhile, the responsibility for hatching the eggs belongs to the male. He uses his pectoral fins to 'fan' water into the nest, improving the oxygen supply. He adds sand to strengthen the structure, and drives other small animals from the vicinity.

After developing for five days, the black eyes of

the embryo are very obvious. The heart can be seen in the center of the egg, and the general shape of the embryo, with its coiled tail, is clearly visible. Pigment cells can also be seen.

The eggs hatch on about the ninth day. For the first few days the young sticklebacks stay hidden in the weeds, nourished by the remains of the yolk sack which is attached to the body.

Then they begin to stray farther afield, making an occasional dash to the surface of the water to swallow air. The adult male keeps a close watch on them at this time, vigorously attacking anything that wanders near the nest. There are many creatures like dragonfly nymphs, who will eat young stickles if given the opportunity.

Gradually, the brilliant color of the adult male starts to fade. His protective instincts begin to wane. About ten days after hatching, the young sticklebacks leave the area.

The adult male, free of one family, may then repeat the breeding cycle all over again.

Sticklebacks eat worms, insects and crustacea; and, in turn, are eaten by pike, perch, otters and kingfishers. They mature after about a year, and though some may live for as long as $3\frac{1}{2}$ years, few survive for more than 18 months.

The photographs you are about to see show the stickleback magnified many, many times by use of special cameras and techniques.

This is the male stickleback. It has three spines.

At breeding time the male has a bright red throat.

Males have fights with each other over their breeding territory.

The male digs out a nest for the female

and collects weed for it.

He then prods the weed into position.

The nest is now ready for this pregnant female.

The male goes through the nest to check that all is well.

Then he courts the female, zigging and zagging around her.

The male points out the nest he has built to the female.

Nudged by the male, she enters the nest.

The female then lays her eggs, which are fertilized by the male.

In the entrance to the nest you can see the female stickleback's eggs.

The female's stomach is now much smaller.

The male uses his front fins to drive fresh water through the nest,

and adds some sand to it with his mouth.

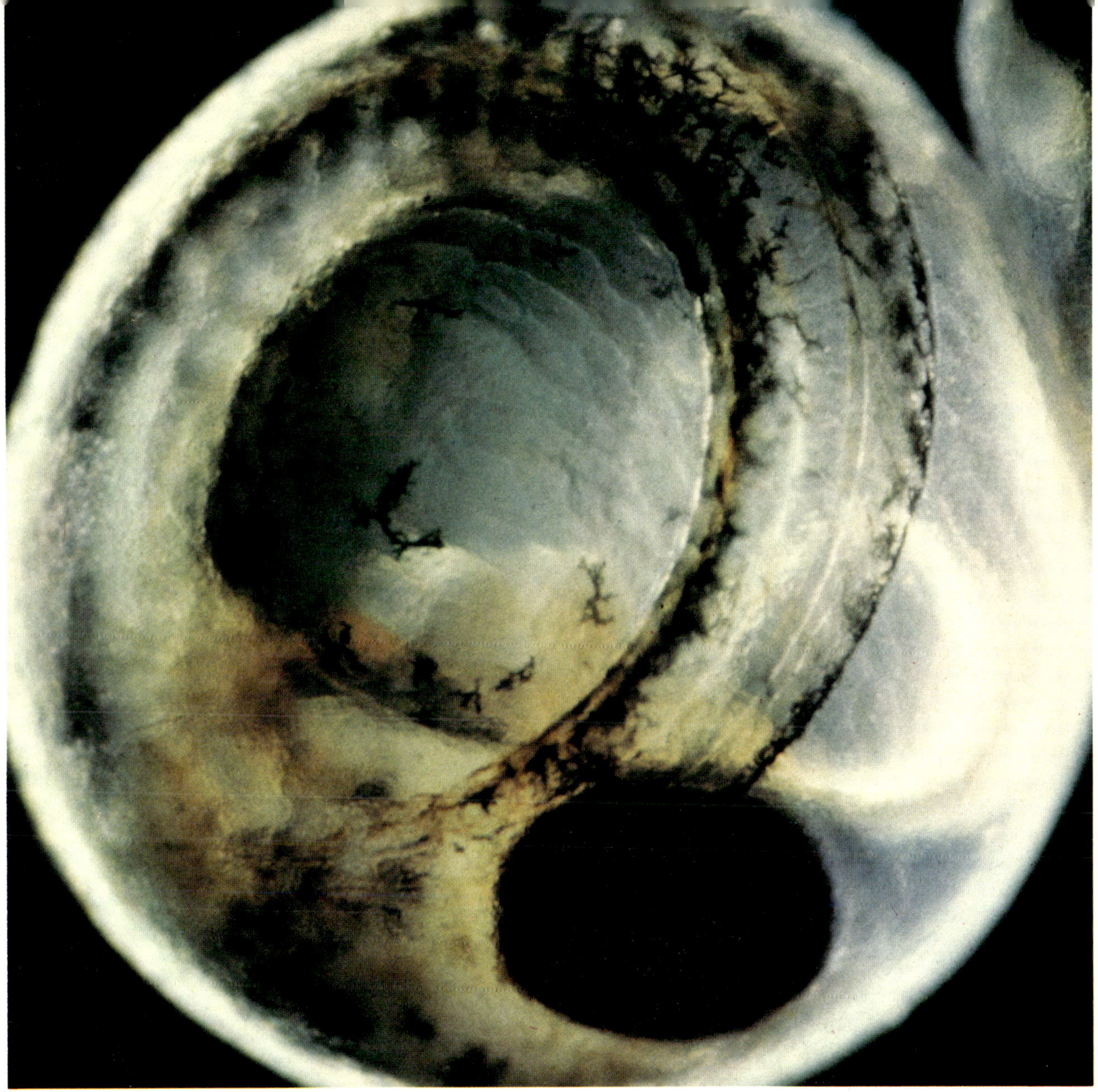

It is five days since the eggs were laid,
and you can see one of the stickleback's eyes.

About four days later the baby stickles hatch.

Because they are young they stay close to the nest, which is guarded by their father.

He scares away possible enemies like this snail,

until the young sticklebacks are big enough to take care of themselves.